The Seasons

The Seasons

Bruce Meyer

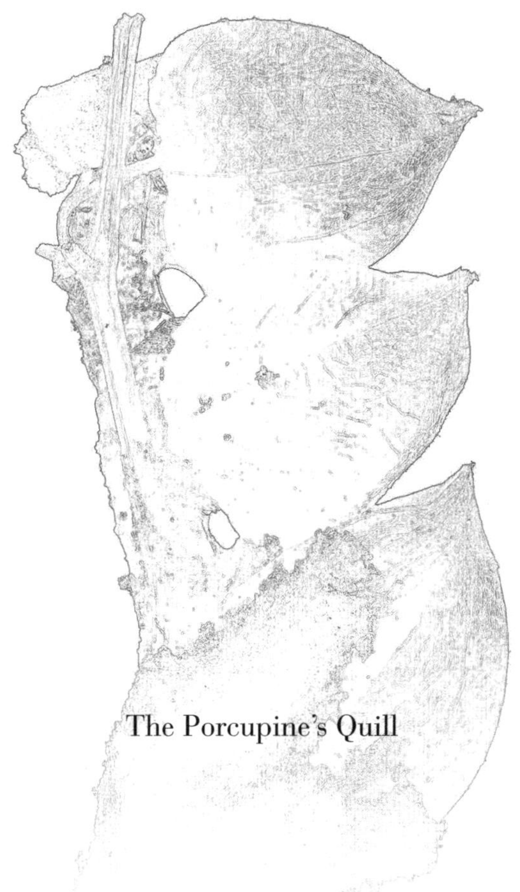

The Porcupine's Quill

Library and Archives Canada Cataloguing in Publication

Meyer, Bruce, 1957–, author
The seasons/Bruce Meyer.

ISBN 978-0-88984-372-1 (pbk.)

1. Seasons—Poetry. 2. Sonnets, Canadian (English).
I. Title.

PS8576.E93S42 2014 C811'.54 C2014-900735-3

1 2 3 • 16 15 14

Published by The Porcupine's Quill, 68 Main Street, PO Box 160, Erin, Ontario NOB 1TO. http://porcupinesquill.ca

Represented in Canada by Canadian Manda Group.
Trade orders are available from University of Toronto Press.

We acknowledge the support of the Ontario Arts Council and the Canada Council for the Arts for our publishing program. The financial support of the Government of Canada through the Canada Book Fund is also gratefully acknowledged.

For Kerry

sólo tu claridad para no seguir siendo
sólo tu amor para cerrar la sombra.

— Pablo Neruda, 'Cien sonetos de amor, XC'

Winter

Seasons have built our lives hour by hour
in the twilight of long, darkening commutes,

and we arrive home too tired to speak of love
and this we say only with a goodnight kiss.

With the sound of the newspaper on the path,
or the grey light between snows peering in,

the cycle begins again, and never ends.
After you have left and before my turn to go,

I sit for a few minutes with a coffee in hand,
the house empty, the silence a cruel reminder

of what life would be like without you here,
and stare at our garden where we grow fine snow.

A painting of frost on the window depicts hands
reaching out to touch. Nature, too, suffers for love.

Just as I am woken by a passing plough
in the middle of the night, I open my eyes

in time to catch its flashing blue light
reflected on the bedroom wall, the engine

grunting, the scoop grating the street bed,
and my dreams are paved like the road

in destinations where I want to see the way ahead,
cleared for us, but that is not the world's way.

If I am lucky enough, the snows will clog
your route to work and we shall spend

the day together, housebound, your voice
filling the silence as if summer returned,

and to assure myself you are still near,
I shuffle my toe to touch your leg until you sigh.

[Assurance]

Not that we can say enough about winter
(not that anyone can), we roll the duvet

from our white bodies and feel the cold
the way the earth must feel the chill

as it waits for that touch of mortal sunlight
to return and tell us there shall be no death

(at least not in the beds of our garden).
Paradise was taken from us the way explanations

retreat like cowards in the face of seasons.
Yet your eyes are windows to the future,

pages of a calendar where I can read ahead
to that blank page where spring begins,

and the days of the past are crossed off
and nothing hangs on those crosses but sunlight.

[Calendar]

Do you remember the first time we kissed?
In front of the posh hotel. You wore a crown

of snow on the red wool scarf that draped
your head; you were my Madonna of the snows

and the whiteness of your skin and the red
of the scarf spoke a purity that filled my heart

as if a blessing. And the whiter the world
became, the purer you made it seem, your breath

forming spheres where spirits danced, singing
your praises … or was it just the passing cars,

their tires melodious on the dark, wet street?
A truck idled and drowned your words, but I knew

there had to be a God and April somewhere
when I looked into the green light of your eyes.

[The Red Scarf]

Without realizing I had slept so long
and the early Sunday afternoon light

was a splendour reminding me of your hair
and the memory of brilliance in the maples,

I heard piano music from the room below.
Every note, a piece I could not name,

was filled with the resonance of walnut
the way wind and sunlight once blew

through its solemn boughs a century ago
when it stood with solid grace among

its fellow trees and thought its only music
was the song of birds or its steadiness

planted firmly in the lowland Ontario soil.
And now your music rises and sleepers wake.

☛ [Piano Music]

What began in darkness and retold itself
in the narrative of hearts we never want to end

is the story of our days and how they multiply
until we cannot remember the lives we've lived

and recall only the patterns of our seasons
that we read over and over each long year

to the point where we hear each other's shadows.
I want to find the words that bring the joy

of an hour with you, the ecstasy of a minute,
and the pleasure of the silence in a clock's tick

when the image of you flashes through my mind
the way a star, almost invisible to the naked eye,

shines constantly to touch its silent emptiness,
where a wish falls to earth if we could catch it.

[Meteor]

Our days are swallowed as if in mouthfuls.
The foundation of time is kept in minutes.

Our rooms fill with unquestioned dust.
The foundation of living dwells in ashes.

Each breath moves us closer to the wind.
The foundation of weather is in whispers.

What we see in daylight leads to night.
The foundation of vision rests in shadows.

Here is my monument to you on paper.
The foundation of eternity is words.

Our garden struggles beneath the snow.
The foundation of dreams rises out of sleep.

I struggle to imagine all our tomorrows.
The foundation of love is merely patience.

❧ [Building Blocks]

We travelled the northern road through fog:
Webbwood emerging among rocks and trees

in a cloud of contradiction—the snow greying
yet melting in the New Year's sudden thaw,

and trailings of anticipatory green emerging
temptingly along the bends of Serpent River.

Our winter journey to Elliot Lake was cold
and sleepy as the history hidden in the shield;

shafts where only hard work surfaced every day,
miners' eyes buried from darkness to darkness

so the world would have light to live and love by;
but you harvested the sun. Your love is energy.

As I looked at you within that grey miasma,
I wrote this by the glow of your voice.

[Uranium]

The first Christmas in our own home,
we spent the holiday together in bed.

Phone off the hook, the lights turned out,
our families thought we had flown away.

We had. In the silence of each other's arms
we soared to worlds we only dream of,

and waking we shared the places we'd been,
the house an ark containing the world,

as we waited paired for winter to pass
and passing hours with the gift of time.

The middle of one night we woke to silence,
and through venetians saw new-fallen snow,

our snow, a land beautiful, a miracle covering
our haven, a blanket wrapping us in our love.

[Hibernation]

Think of all the things that cannot love us.
The blond stubble of last year's flowers

rising from the powder of the year's first snow
afloat as if survivors of a once proud ship

bobbing in sea-foam and awaiting rescue.
Sail on. Storm clouds that trees once held,

straining as if to hold back the falling sky,
cast shadow veins in memory of blood

to remind us that we live and die to live
and fear what cannot love us like ourselves.

Driving today, the road curtained white ahead,
we saw the veil of God descend upon us,

and refused His hand; the love of our skin,
yours on mine, is the only promise we can keep.

[The Veil]

We are the audience of snow falling in the light
the way a street lamp watches every flake,

the angle of the drift, the force of wind,
an updraft, a sudden lull, the choreography

of a million white birds on tired wings.
Stand with me at the window now. Watch

as the storm becomes a migration of snow geese,
an open duvet in flight, a pillow burst with laughter.

Changes wrought by heaven bow the pines,
a yellow grey in the sky growing brighter

as the night is suddenly warmer, and darker,
and the backlight of horizon is a rush of dancers.

And when the falling ceases, the house grows
dark to the sound of one-handed applause.

[Ballet]

The snow is making its own light tonight
by the brilliance of its fall from heaven.

Every flake, every angel cry for help,
is bright enough before its melting

to fill the street, the trees, our bedroom window
with angelic splendour to light your face.

I see the reflection fluttering in your eyes,
that sigh with seraphim breaths exhaled

by the heaven hidden inside your dreams.
We are so alone in this moment of humanity,

and I would not wake you for sapphire streets
paved with all the diamonds in the snow.

But watch your eyes become delicate wings
knowing that in heaven we are exquisite jewels.

❧ [Let the Bright Seraphim]

As late morning, late afternoon, and late hope
flood in gradual tarnish through our window,

I pass the unmade bed where our spirits rose
as dawn's snows hissed against the panes.

Engraved upon white sheets like prints
made by sparrows when the falling ended,

the outlines of our bodies imprinted
where we lay, one fitting round the other.

Is this our benchmark of happiness, top arm
reaching to seize something dear yet fading,

the hollow of heads and hips and legs curled
one number in another adding up to two?

Are we equal to the calculations of time?
I shiver and bless each day I count with you.

[Winter Numbers]

You look up from your keyboard
to share a joke or a news story,

or in the middle of our travels
you turn and tell me something new.

You are my teacher, moderator, kind
ear, the silent voice in all our narrative:

for what defines us is what we do,
so that by every laugh, every look

we are one, sharing the electric moment.
The dawn of every day prepares me

for the lessons of your thought. I am
your passionate pupil, pen in hand,

ready to take note of what you say.
Teach me, and I shall pass the human test.

[The Pupil]

When I see you disappearing
down the front walk at dawn

or open my eyes thinking that I hear
the car engine start in the drive

my heart sinks and the spirit in me
vanishes with you into darkness.

As the sun comes up over fields
where late harvest ploughings left

traces of long winter storms
still cradled in unseeded fingers

and your breath hovers as a promise
when you step down to the platform,

I long to be a shadow in the crowd
that brushes gently against your shadow.

Flannel leaves more to the imagination
than silks or satins against smooth skin.

It tells me that just as in all great art
the mind must be engaged in discovery,

that the curves of your body are uncharted
and my hands will trace my thoughts—

that when I close my eyes I see a goddess
hidden beneath your warm-skinned smile.

It is cold outside. The wind is howling.
It claws at the house and whines to come in.

It merely wants to be warm at last—
to slip its hand inside your button front

and dream of paradise and tropical light
as a navigator kisses land on his arrival.

The beauty of cold nights is the way
we have of knowing how to stay warm.

The house is eaten by cold. We hear its bones
crack in the jaws of sub-zero. Such nights

define the stars. Clear, cold nights revealing
stars we had not noticed, some shooting,

riding the atmosphere to brilliance, a focus
that permits us to peer deeply into the universe.

On the far side of time and space we see
the shape of tomorrows waiting for us,

sunrises and sunsets as the world turns away.
Draw close to me tonight. Your warmth

is a constellation of bright seas of life.
I am a navigator and you my constant star.

[Celestial]

If these words were dying snowflakes
and never meant to last beyond a breath,

if every thought were but a tiny paper boat
floating on the long green river of time …

if every heartbeat were but an echo sounding
to plead for an answer that cannot be heard …

we would still believe in the livid spring
that drives us to the melting of our touch.

We would overlook the pallid certainty
that what is here will always be

and how defeat leads to a better victory
and each heartbeat is a season's door to more …

You'd think a moment happens and is over,
but each is a beginning and an end we cannot see.

[Heartbeats]

No footstep goes unnoticed. We trace a journey
in the divinity of winter to search for life.

The park across the street is blue in the sunlight,
the air is perfumed with a purity we breathe.

Sunlight could steal this moment, but not yet.
If you put your hand in the heart of the fallen sky

remember it is a catalogue of our memories,
your touch, a recollection through fallen time—

for what numbs us is neither time nor loss
nor even loss of love, but the petals of the sky's blossom

strewn on our sleeping garden; and this paradise,
sleeping as a flower sleeps in hardened earth,

is a memorial of how I long to touch you,
to feel the spring pulsing through your hands.

[Snow Garden]

Our footprints in the freshly fallen snow
show us where we have been. Blue shadows

lengthen in our strides, throwing back on us
the image of ourselves, fresh holly boughs

in our hands to guide us through the netherworld
where death sparkles with diamond brightness

and shines on us like a promise we cannot keep.
Thus, we say, here is the story of our lives,

the tracks pointing to the place we stand
and desire to know this whispered moment:

we kiss, a sonnet shared between us in a cloud
as a chickadee scolds us for our presence.

And the life in the red berries runs wild,
and the blood of uncertain history is on our hands.

[Holly]

Our daughter served us sandwiches
that had been chilled in a snowbank

metres from our front door. With banks
shoulder high, we lay in the hollow

she had carved with seats and shelves,
and had our winter picnic beneath stars.

She had never seen so much snow. Breath
became dragons, and riddles questions

where we knights dressed in snow clothes
ate a banquet of our days. It was a feast.

The table is spread before us with joy
that is as fresh as minty air, yet numb

to freeze moments we are truly happy—
each mouthful melting as we phrase it.

[Snow Picnic]

Our garden became a saint's reliquary
after the ice storm passed; behind glass

rests divinity in roses and holiness in twigs.
On the shingles rivulet tadpoles beneath a veil

writhe like snakes into the icicled eavestrough
and from the trees shards of broken glass

fall as if the spheres themselves shattered
and we were called upon to catch their music.

This is what paradise must have seemed
in the days after the fall: heaven weeping.

The world remaining, still, with holy patience,
dwelt in a timeless rose-scented rebirth, at the ready

to rise in glory, uncorrupted, full of knowledge
death is only momentary and love unbroken sleep.

[Reliquary]

Try not to think the stars this winter night
are sparks that rose from our last bonfire

we set beside the lake that August evening.
Yes, we made them from the crafted fire,

watched as they flew skyward to join
their fellow promises among the constellations

and took the names of mythical heroes
from legends not yet told and wishes

not yet made. Tonight, our exhausted breaths
are fires spent and cooled as if smoke rising

in the limitless clarity of the February sky
where everything freezes to the stillness of its soul,

and I say to you, *hold tight*, as we wheel
into tomorrow armed only with our dreams.

[Bonfire]

And so, off the main highway
as the journey moves us forward

we pass those clapboard houses
built more than a century ago

in the silent isolation of fields
newly cleared and still shivering

where snow billows drifted blindly
for the first time and could not stop.

Anna Jameson wrote of seeing lights
glowing in the paired front windows

as if they were windows to the soul,
staring off into the darkness believing

that summer would someday return
as we believe we will always be young.

[Old Houses]

As we bend together to admire
the crystal goblets in the cabinet

the mirror of the glass frames
our faces in each small prism.

The clear-cut lines, the rainbows
of light thrown back in portrait

transform us into pure illusions,
the optics of eternal promises,

light we shall become someday
when our spirits have been consumed.

What shall we taste like to the future?
Shall we be bitter on the tongue,

or sweet and complex, a melody,
as they drain each glass to find us?

[Crystal]

Spring

After a long winter as the skeletal trees
appear from labyrinths of scattered shadows

looking fragile, unsteady as morning risers,
a few small scrub oak, bent and pale

clutch their remaining white-haired leaves
that even through winter they refused to relinquish

the way we hold the hallmark of our years.
Amid patches of snow the ground guards,

you remark the scrub oaks look like me
having outlived my winters, my hair white.

But you are the birch beside and a dance
of trilliums will bloom to sing your praises

the way angels in the bright Empyrean
gather in the beauty of what is always now.

[Birch]

We drove into the countryside believing
that the first warm day of the new spring

could last forever if we went far enough.
We stood among small islands of snow

watching the headland of Nottawasaga
curve northward to the west as waves

forever faithful the way the heart is faithful
for an entire lifetime kept their steady beat.

The lives of everything we know are measured
in illusions—time, wind, sand, love,

and of these only love will survive the rest
as the last ray of sunshine in our seasons

hangs on the last hem of a distant star
to light the world with the stories of our lives.

[Fictions]

That patch where you carved your garden
for basil and chives and Chinese parsley

will soon re-emerge from the snow
the way a patient has a miraculous cure

and steps, almost newborn, from his sheets.
And when the time arrives, you will plant it

with the same faith and muddy hands
you've used to paint our garden green.

Bleeding hearts will yield to lilies,
roses will announce themselves again,

and life will sit on the tips of our tongues,
a whisper to describe how we lived through winter.

All things being equal, you will give us hope.
How we make it work is what we live for.

[Equinox]

It is fitting that the cold rain at dawn
washed away most of the lawn's snow,

exposing the raw earth, the scent of life
or death, or both, with the inkling of grass.

This is a sad day, a day to remember
a victory, a battle won at a huge cost.

No one pauses to reflect, yet I remember,
the weight the way memory tells us

that our lives were also built by others
who knew we would struggle, work,

and live to keep faith with love.
Our lives, even on this day in history

permit us to close our eyes and weep,
as fingerling shoots rise to imitate our hands.

[History]

Thinking of that fine-scented restaurant
on the rue St. Louis and how cobbles

always tilted us closer into each other
as we walked in the frigid spring air

in search of moonlight and memories
I open a bottle of red I've cellared

like a rosary bead with a prayer I forget
and try to find a saint to intercede for us.

But there are sudden flights to life:
flying over snow geese in migration;

the way a candle burns shorter than expected;
and sun growing vaster in the days ahead,

lit by miracles of life returned to life
passing this frail gift of love between us.

[Triduum]

We had driven out at sunset
past that crossroads named for prayer

to find some open ground for the dog
to run the day off pent up inside her.

At the edge of the small fairgrounds,
she leapt into the cinder parking lot,

and tossing her glowing yellow ball,
we watched her vanish in darkness.

I will never give up hope as long as you
stand beside me just as you did then,

holding our breaths, waiting for the moment
the small, yellow light of summer

gallops toward us, panting and eager,
with life held firmly in its clench.

Some days I think of our marriage
as a flying island propelled by angels.

Around the cliffs and scenic lookouts
where for fifty cents with stereoscopes

you can gaze across expansive lands,
clouds wash ashore in billowed waves

while we rise beyond them in deep night
drawn close enough to feel their gleam.

Everything that holds us floating here
is made of wishes and toughened prayers,

the spirit-dreams souls dream together
when dreaming seems absurd as steady ground—

for there is no science that keeps us flying
though love is what keeps our angels fed.

[Laputa]

Spring is measured in things that fly.
The blackflies come first for our flesh,

solemn communicants of life who seek
the resurrection of their bodies, the host

that loves them until no love remains.
Next, the mosquitoes whose taste for blood

is a craving for rebirth, the music of life
alive in our ears when life runs red,

the agony, temptation, the sting of eternity,
pang as reminder of our beliefs. I believe,

finally, as spring dries to summer, flying things
are the work of divine inspiration, open souls

asking for love or attention. Martyred
on the wall, they sought our absolution.

On the night of the first day of spring
we opened the upper windows of the house

and let air into the hall ways of our lives.
The night was moist with warm breath,

and through sunken clouds bright Venus
shone with a magic that cast shadows

on the art books of the upper corridors.
Beauty is when we entertain the cosmos

in the comfort of our own home, when the eternal
comes into our lives framed or unframed;

it is rare, delicate, a yellow light on spines;
the books, your back, a glow transforming you

before my eyes into the work of art you are;
and I behold you now, and frame you in words.

[Venus]

The women at our wedding wore large hats.
The brim shadows falling on their smiles

reminded me of violets shaded by trees
or tiger lilies on the lip of a grove

alive and whispering heaven into trilliums.
Looking deeper in the moment of their smiles.

I saw the happiness they felt for you,
the way I looked deeply into your eyes

and saw our lives reflected in a May morning,
sunlight through branches coined for blessing,

a wedding gift that came without a card.
Something in the universe must love us deeply.

If I could find words for lives such as these,
I pledge them to you until my heart blossoms too.

[Straw Hats]

The closer we grow to learning who we are
the more we puzzle over what made us.

Poring over records in Sainte-Cécile-de-Masham,
parchments in lost tongues still so familiar,

or sifting through archives grain by grain
in hope of finding that diamond in the Gatineaus,

we realized we are only what we made
of ourselves, the vanishing story of our voices.

And that night we pledged each to each
as ancestors for future eyes awaiting faces,

we lay down with our history, awestruck
that someone might someday reckon us,

and planting a seed in the overgrown forest
consider we were saplings reaching up for light.

[Ancestor Dance]

Paradise must have had the echo of a chill
in the air as it sprang to life that first day

and the wind, excited to be alive and warm,
blossomed on the tips of twig forsythia

and in childlike expectation was forever new.
The golden age emerged from winter chaos

as a voice declaring the existence of light,
and I put my hand to your smooth pink cheek

where the warmth settled as if a soft bird
that returned to the place where it was hatched.

We are here, in that garden where spring began
as if it had never begun before. Your smile

that seemed only a promise of creation last night
emerged *ex nihilo*, and your green eyes say *life*.

[Your Smile]

The Lord loves what we do not see,
His vision so particular, so infinite

that ministers of light lose touch
with the bright reality of horizons.

And where He put his fingers in the rock
and filled such places with His grace

the ice has left the living world as breath
to sing the resurrected spirit beyond death.

Holy is the great imagined sepulchre
from which the stone of long delay is rolled,

for in all our being and its long desire
there is evidence of things not seen,

and wings of geese as bright as morning
rise to greet us as day greets night.

[Good Friday, Driving North]

As we climbed the rocky street in your hometown,
walking among the lighted evening windows

of miners' houses laid on a rolling landscape
that would not lie down for settlement's sake,

a round sun-burst moon, as full of promise
as if it had written us a letter on behalf of summer,

reared up in the purple night sky, startled Venus,
and made Jupiter sink slowly on the horizon.

Across the valleys intertwined like fingers clasped
in the hands of strolling lovers such as us,

the lights of houses dotted the pined hillside
in a constellation named for distant heroes.

May they all look upon us now, as I gaze
in awe at the loveliness I worship in your eyes.

[Full Spring Moon]

When I was a child I would feel the sea
struggling to move my feet in sand,

the tug of wash, some distant insistence
of control demanding its way with passion,

the way anger rises in your voice and life
becomes a shout rather than a whisper.

The best thing is to say nothing, stay dry,
let the waves calm down; but the sea days

are where we craft our lives with change.
For all their suffering, kingfishers laugh

at turning tides and what the sea gives them;
and if I wait long enough they turn again

as the sun follows the moon, sparkling
where we voyage on the calm of whispers.

[Kingfishers]

Tonight I fell asleep beside you with the cap
loose on my fountain pen, and when I woke

the sky had turned to ink and only the moon
came clean when I scraped it with my finger.

To let some light in before you stirred
and could scold me for being careless,

I punched a myriad of tiny holes above us,
but these were mere reminders of the stars.

So I apologize for what I wrote in sleep,
and to make amends I give more precious ink

to one whose beauty fills the night with words
and dreams only a fool would not profess;

who guides my soul down rivers of ink
to arrive at your praise, paddling with my pen.

[Serendipity]

One spring I went on a journey without you.
Sadly, I left you, the baby, the house, the time

of sunset and daybreak. I crossed the ocean
and slept, dreaming of your day still ticking,

your footsteps on the oak floors of home,
the rhythm of your routine as twilight chimed.

The distant city was timeless, the hotel faceless.
In the corridors I heard cogs of people pass,

their conversation broken and fading softly.
Lights flooded eternal monuments, pigeons

sat inscrutable upon great bronze giants,
and time was empty without you to see it.

I returned—you and the baby on our front walk:
time began for me with the bloom of your smile.

[Forsythia]

Hotels in mid-afternoon are a library
of labyrinth corridors with nothing to read

where a bull-headed muse might wander
after the maids have departed with laundry

and left only a polished silence sleeping.
Here is a place where I hear you breathing.

The white afternoon light through draperies
illuminates the puzzle of travel and arrival,

a soft bed, a comfortable pillow, a duvet
beneath which others have hidden before

being called onwards at their thread's end.
We are travellers attempting to shed our purpose,

exhausted from discovery, hiding behind doors,
and waiting to confront what hides within us.

[Hotel I]

Passion is a stray ember that rose
from the burning shore across the lake

and attached itself to the loveless dark
that cowered over us and sank itself,

reflectionless, in the still waters below.
We would open our window wide as a cry

to let the breath of eternity embrace us
in our huddled place, but the blue smoke,

that incense of what is lost in purity,
tries to choke us, and our promises

and whispers are more important to us
than any hope of touching distant stars.

But my love, smoke was your nightgown
and when I whispered your name it vanished.

[The Forest Fire]

There are days when it is hard to believe
the world is as real as it claims to be.

The sun struggles with a chill that remains,
the chill answers *it is impossible to die.*

Everything runs its course yet comes again.
We offer prayers for life and resurrection

knowing that what we leave behind returns.
A stray cat has padded into the backyard

and rubs itself against my leg. I complain
that I would rather it was you caressing me.

You rose this morning, departed, leaving
the scent of your hair on the pillow beside me.

And yet, I imagine your return, like spring,
the birds, and that needy cat. Brush by me with life.

Let us lie together before daybreak
and watch the contours of our bodies

in the first whispers of light. Let us take
solace that we form a landscape countries

would be envious of, a place of hearts
beating silently against the dying night

where every raised hand or hope starts
the process of declaration that might

lead to independence and all we dream of—
a place where every bird in the dawn

of dreams takes wing because to fly is love,
the love that peoples nations, the love drawn

from constitutions of unwavering compassion
the love that transforms landscapes into lovers.

[Birdsong]

A chevron of geese signals victory
against a sunset of orange and gold;

they are heading north and the sky
is a refraction of the relinquished hold

that tried to choke life from our breath.
Winter besieged us. Every word a cloud

hovered as we spoke; the angel of death
looked over our shoulder and told

us we were nothing. We remain, and here
and now, as if a smile had suddenly broken

on your face, that sound that last year
signalled winter's onset. Kerry, life has spoken.

Look up, it says. The world is finally waking.
I return your smile though it was mine for taking.

[Wild Geese]

I have a picture of you standing
on stairs that pass through rock

almost as if you emerged from rock
and the Elora Gorge dropping below

falls away like the image's edge
when memory says *mine forever.*

You are wearing your flowered dress,
the roses emerging from rock the way

life emerges from death or your face
emerges from the blur of memories

and dark silences that cloud the eye;
I want to think of you smiling at me;

the way it might have been for Orpheus,
a smile worth a million songs and more.

☛ [The Hole]

We drove that little white rental car
until it turned grey with Northern dust

of rock cuts and side roads among lakes.
The trees tried to shield themselves

from the glare of western sunlight
as we motored into the Joseph's coat

of sunsets and enamelled afterglows stilling
the horizon as we watched for moose.

The first berries had ripened in the days
numbered before our departure and their colour,

a rich hue of sunsets and sunsets to come,
enticed us until blueberries filled the car

with the perfume and sweetness of a love
that maps travellers beneath a blueberry sky.

Beside our door stood two sad pines,
two old guardians in hanging clothes

who witnessed our comings and goings,
who stood silently through winter snows

and bore time with a saintly patience.
If their arms were uplifted, you would say

they were celebrants of love who danced
to the evenings and beats of our days.

But their shadow: they almost mirrored
us, standing watch over the path that led

to those places in our hearts where our
silence was the silence of time that fed

desires and planted hopes of the future
in a sleeping garden, seeding our days to come.

[The Guardians]

Summer

You are there in roses and in raindrops,
the reflection of sunlight in still windows,

in the mist that hugs a field at dawn
or the last thoughts of stars at daybreak;

your whispers in breath on winter mornings,
or a lake we feel between our toes,

or in empty rooms that time our hearts
or the silence of shadows on a wall;

you whisper in the library of my memories
and flip through pages of my favourite book;

or call me the way an ocean calls us
when the far horizon seems so familiar

I know I've been there a million times,
reclined on its beach and listened to time.

[You]

You say the sound of crickets in the night
makes you wake and listen to their song

as if they are trying to teach us about love.
The air begins to sweat its solemn matins,

and before dawn becomes humid as breath
I awaken to the dark conversation,

air gradually cooling around our bodies
and silence is about to say something true.

I am wondering if you are wondering
how the soul finds its way through hours

when the world wants to remind us of who
and what we are and how time masters

every moment and holds us anxiously
saying 'one more breath and then another'.

[Sleeping with the Window Open]

Only a fool would dream of riches
when what is rarest are moments

I spend with you. They have no price.
Each one is rare. Each one a jewel.

Driving out through the Oro highlands
we could sense the gold of our country,

the gems of hidden in Simcoe Forests,
the trees standing like terracotta warriors

in silent rows guarding an emperor's hoard,
the pot of gold at the end of the rainbow.

When you tell me stories the road through
my memory is paved with more and more

and among birches scattering coins of light
you make me the wealthiest man alive.

[Riches]

In my notebook I carry a picture of you
standing in a water-carved passageway

cut through limestone in Elora Gorge,
tunnelling its questions through ancient seas.

The same sun that lights your green eyes
greeted the mason species at their birth,

its rays stoking the salty drive of life
I felt the moment I raised my camera

and knew I would make a future with you,
the way oceans and great reefs made life.

When we are stone will the world recall us?
Your dress, printed with burgundy flowers,

their stems swirled and intertwined as minutes
shall be discovered: a fossil blooming in the stone.

☛ [Eurydice]

Honeycomb in limestone is almost sweet,
and fans of ancient coral or hidden shoals

whisper secrets we heard only in pearl shells.
Seas once washed this island to its bone,

and creatures left their bodies bleaching,
one atop the other, beneath tropical noons.

This afternoon the sun is playing tricks again.
It is glistening in a myriad of tiny gems

no more precious than salt. The rocks thirst.
A flock of geese chevron overhead. Light

shatters into diamonds for drowning fools.
And night comes as it always has. We listen.

Soon this island will drown again.
Our days together are summer light on waves.

[Fossils]

Lying on the dock with our hands cupped
around our faces to shade our eyes

from the moon's bright glow, we watch
as stars and distant galaxies converse

silently amongst themselves sharing secrets
of what they know from having watched

our lives. Some have peered in our window
as we gently melded into one, whispering

the beauty of smooth skin in silken darkness
the way lake waters recite lyrics to the shore—

and in an instant our lives are further bound
together, as if they hadn't been that way forever,

as we watch a shooting star flare bright blue,
reach it, catch it, a part of tomorrow's sky.

[Perseids]

Putting your hand in mine, our fingers knit,
you taught me the bones and valleys of rock

that became my land because it was yours;
how to hold north wind in my empty palm

and warm it until it became a fragile bird
rising to a thunderhead to spread its wings.

Sometimes I felt constellations in your touch
and sometimes I closed my eyes to comprehend

the night dancing with green and orange haunting
the horizon and stroking the moon's rough skin;

and when you let go I knew daybreak was near
the way we reached out and touched in darkness

as if we made a pledge to be one and only one
when there was nothing to touch except our souls.

[Aurora Borealis]

Our first summer together of raspberries
and blueberries stained our hands,

and when our palms clasped red and blue
the warmth of each finger intertwined was sweet

and royal with the secret purple we held.
At the highest point of land above your town

you knelt among the canes and thickets,
your smile stained the colour of clear sky;

and when I kissed your lips the perfume
of summer among the granite outcrops

told me that life was in us both the way
even the smallest cleft in stone bears gifts,

a branch held out from lifelessness to give
a gift of life, a hand offering us blue pearls.

[Canes]

Milton said the world was a tiny bauble
suspended from heaven as a pendant.

Yesterday I spoke with my mother in Paris.
Today, I see you lying beside a northern lake

like Odysseus cast upon Phaeacian shores.
This is a small planet, a jewel like you,

a place encyclopedic as a perfect snowflake,
shining like the sails of a distant skiff

upon a sunlit lake toned in this world's hue.
I am sitting too close to a bird's nest, a box

someone has hung upon a tree, its own garden,
a creator's promise, a maker's sacrifice to life.

He scolds and I obey his nattered commands.
I want to keep this moment a paradise for all.

[Nuthatch]

Though they are silent as clocks
awaiting the hour when the wind

will give them momentary voice,
you know they keep their secrets.

A spider climbs between the pipes,
turning his web because he knows

the season, like our time together,
is far too short for anything but life.

Love, if you examine his web you find
husks of winged things that danced,

filling the air with anxious wings,
and just out of reach their freedom

as clear as time and just as cold
and the chime to vespers between them.

[Spider in the Wind Chimes]

The eyelets on the flagpole clanged all day
as if they were cymbals in an ancient dance,

and north wind as if a shout of joy
chased clouds down the channel's sleeve.

As we stand here on the shingle beach,
kites caught in the sky's slate expanse,

clasp hands; spread your wingless arms,
and look at stars, more infinite and constant

as a gust of wind reminds how time began
exploding above us, the Milky Way spilled.

Our breaths are small and helpless as birds
returning to their nests from whitecaps.

Your hand is cold in my small hand;
let me warm it with all my life.

[Starlit]

The light of a full, bright moon shatters
on the glass surface of South Bay channel

and becomes a million moons with open mouths
hungry to devour the night the way that face

of fear in the moon struck awe in the heavens
with a wide, famished mouth to swallow stars.

The fry have risen to the surface to feed,
their voracious, tiny mouths gulping light

that feeds them when mosquitoes have flown
and that torrid hunger possesses all things.

In the darkness, side by side, the window open,
a soft breeze heavy with midnight dampness,

we stare into each other's eyes, a blanket of air
upon us, and feed delicately on each other's lips.

[The Fry]

When our daughter was a little girl
she had a round, inflatable yellow boat

that bore a duck's head proudly forward
and stood out like sunshine on waves.

We tried taking turns huffing our lungs
into the balloon-brained creature, all so

it would float, spread its wings to fly,
and bob gently in ripples near the shore.

Today I watched a flock of mallards,
mother and eight hatchlings, floating by

as you sat reading on the dock, the world
of written words captivating you completely

as the inflated sun flapped its midday wings
and I breathed into it the inspiration of love.

[The Yellow Duck]

I have been waiting to share a rainy day
with you for years—a time when the lake

greys over, when damp fills the pages we read
and alters every word into soft silence;

when the cottage walls become pines again
and almost spread their forgotten arms

to catch the short-lived blessing of peace.
I have waited to hear your breaths exhale

between the distant claps of eastern thunder
that have hushed the intrusive city inside us,

learning, just there, our thoughts drift
to a place where we drown in the music

of sky flowing from roof, to shore, to lake,
and the unseen ocean our hearts beat for.

Poetry can never be about indifference.
It is too much like love. It attaches

itself to things one either wants to say,
cannot say, or should have said long ago.

It lies awake in the darkness and replays
the day still alive inside it, pulls the covers

close around its heart, and listens intensely
for the breath of the lover, those heartbeats

hidden in words it would speak for me
to tell you how much I miss you

when we are not together and cannot
share or joke or pass a story between us

with such adamant phrases and eloquent
gestures we almost learn by heart.

❧ [Ars Poetica]

There are myths of how we came by fire,
but none of how we harnessed water,

and when we arrived home one night
to find a lake where our basement lay,

the question of telling stories was moot.
Your guitar floated like a wooded island

and the isle was full of noises; some books
were drowned but we abjured no magic;

and we survived that tempest, the drains
dug up, our house spirited by workmen.

Poets and artists have died by water,
their inspirations overwhelmed, their words

sunken where they wrote their names; but O,
castaway! Love cast it away and waters parted.

[Shipwrecked]

Imagine the odds that we should wake together
as the sun pours through our picture window

and sitting up in bed, still groggy and confused,
tell each other of the places we just dreamed.

Imagine that when we share these foggy secrets
the dreams are identical and we went together

to that place where not even gods can go,
the centre of each other's being walled off,

and walking in that garden, that *hortus conclusus*
conjured by a timeless desire we both share,

we set foot in Eden and all of time stood still.
The alarm clock never rang. Animals lay beside us,

and your beautiful body shining with such light
made all things new, and made me new in you.

[The Awakening]

You can write it in any colour of ink
and though the words will be the same

the shadow of the sun or absence of light
will walk across the page like shadows

and startle you as birds do when suddenly
they appear on the windowsill and sing.

Love knows no colours though a red
is always marked for passion and green

is the reflection of summer in your thoughts.
Yellow is for sunlight and memories

though it is hard to read and turns to sky
the longer you cast your eyes to read.

But these words are meant only for you
in midnight's silent shade. They are my whispers.

[Inks]

You wore the hard light of summer morning
as I towelled glistening droplets from your skin

and your round, full shoulders sloped
as if white Killarney hills smoothed

to statue marble by the beauty they express,
the lives they have lived. We go on together

being landscapes in the map of our stories,
and by night, as the Perseids fall in sparks

of the shattered music that was heaven,
I wonder if they landed where we swim,

and if I have dried one tiny star on you.
Let me be clothed in your spirit nakedness,

in the light of the sun streaming from you
the way all living things drink the fallen sky.

❧ [Towelling Off]

You come to me some nights
the way a story enters the mind

before it has found a voice to tell it.
A place, perhaps a lakeside dock

late on a dusty summer afternoon
as geese paddle leisurely to nest

and the sun calms into the stillness
where tired light goes out to rest—

that place is where the story begins
as a touch of wind moving your hair

and it is a whisper I hear again
at night with the window open

and the moonlight watches us together,
you in my arms describing forever.

[The Story]

My heart is an island in the channel
and wind pulsing through scrivener pines

is an allegory of my pen on the page for you.
Each line is the channel's current in a word;

each dark cloud patch on water is my ink,
and in muffling wind you hear my whispers.

Our cheeks blush in the racing wind. We learn
from the volumes of experience we share.

My heart, my soul, you wrap me like the wind.
You speak to me in the weather of late summer.

When what I must learn of life is so urgent,
so real, you remind me these are flying days

and with good reason. The clouds roar past.
They run toward the love we've yet to know.

[The Flying Days]

Summer is only mortal and the pain
of watching it slow down to roads

where the dust rises in our tired path
home in the dying Sunday supper light

is more than I can bear. I feel as if
we are driving to the end of our lives

and it is too painful to speak of more.
Already the grasshoppers are leaping.

An earth-treader on my arm as I loaded the car
gave me pause for the imperfection of wishes,

the eternal summer that shall not fade,
and the maturing absence of everlasting youth.

Share this silence home with me now.
Every wish is but half the answer we desire.

[Grasshopper]

Just as the sun sets behind the ridge at Grenfel
and the dead settle their bones for another night

in the old cemetery across the moon's long road,
a pair of geese trumpet to the failing light.

If we should find a way out of paradise,
a small aperture through which we might slip

in order to explore the ways life and purpose,
we would still return here by stilled stars,

bright Venus shining seductively toward Mars
as the dog barks at their heavenly love to find

a path for wishes in the sky. We are so alone
in this universe with our small dreams,

as night sky wraps itself around the earth.
Wish it be the green blanket on our bed.

[Happy Valley]

I am so tired and yet I can't stop dreaming.
I dream I am inside your dreams and you

in mine. We walk through constellations,
the dog star at the leash's end pulling us

through time to where dreams come true.
This time is our time and yet our moment

has not come. I dream of tomorrows when stars
will shine for us and not just because they glow.

And when I have grown so tired I cannot dream,
as tired as I have grown from putting my shoulder

to the wheel of life and pushing when nothing
seems left to give except my love for you,

your dreams fill mine and I am inspired
the way heroes live forever among stars.

[Dreams]

Someday we shall call goodbye
to life the way we leave for a walk

or parting on the platform after the train
has emptied and crowds flow into the earth.

Perhaps a kiss. Perhaps a glance behind
reminding us of parting on humid mornings

when summer breath was kisses and we could not
leave the night behind. Time will tell.

Time will tell because its shadow follows us—
but ignore it—it is still not all our business.

Life is bliss, the bliss we are blessed to know.
It is a map we are unfolding slowly as we go,

uncertain if it will lead us to treasure but sure
it is our path that love has pledged us to go.

[August]

Autumn

I found a blank page in my notebook,
a space I overlooked the way I forget

the small things you do for me out of love,
the space that is not filled with necessity

but like an empty life longs to be filled.
Love finds such small spaces in the world,

small gaps and crannies in ordinary time
where the story of our lives longs to be told.

A footprint of your walk along the beach
fills with water as the tide comes in,

and in a moment it becomes a small ocean
I look to see new worlds there, the islands

whose names and stories are a map of our souls.
In what time we have, let me discover you.

[Explorers]

This page is the moment we are alive.
It is the colour of your skin by morning

as light floods in the windows to read by
and illumines the lines of your sleeping body

where I search for metaphors of truth and love.
I would turn the page to see if there is more,

but I want to hold this moment as an image
where letters are a V of geese migrating south,

want to know the poetry of your presence
and the rise and fall of your breath as if

everything stood still and beautiful and
is as blank and empty as that white place

we have not yet invented, that moment
we are words upon a page waiting to live forever.

[The Page]

I wish I knew who has held me earthbound,
the detractors whose words are tethers,

whose flightless lives have never known
love's desire to rise to the morning sky

and seek the life that does not die with seasons.
But you, my love, are my wings; your strength

the pull of great migrations, the human cry
to rise despite the bitter arrows of life

and follow the sun's long ride to the far south.
You are the light that washes tropical waves,

the wind that cleanses my soul of tears.
My spirit, you are always with me. I strive

despite the pain in my tired wings.
As long as you are my sun, I persevere.

☛ [Migration]

There must be a language that has a word
for grey skies that hover over empty trees,

a tongue that has licked night from heaven
with words of flame and cleansing passion,

and tasted the salt so like your skin.
Even as we wait for the last leaf's fall,

even as your eyes grow weary and your hair
becomes the colour of leafless branches

strand by single strand and tracery by line,
I still see the brilliance of your smile,

your eyes dancing in a way that falling leaves
cannot hope to earn their angel wings,

the dance that claims what life defies, the music
I hear in your eyes, still green as willow boughs.

[Tongues]

I am always sad to see the fields cut down,
the pale stubble in brown furrows surrendered

as if ground lost in mortal combat; the soldiers
of corn that greeted us in proud russet ranks.

They have vanished in the air, the silence,
the bite of wind on our cheeks. We should not

toil so hard for death; yes, I know, the harvest
is about life; but when you lay your head

upon my shoulder the first night of flannel air
and the ghosts of the dead world rise and call

and I clutch you as tightly and as gently
as love permits, I am filled with sorrow

not merely for the world but for all we love.
I stole this peck of sunlight to anoint your eyes.

[Stubble]

Autumn is the love letter life writes to the world,
knowing its time is short and desiring remembrance.

Autumn pleads for the wolf spider beside our door,
admiring a web the world is the lesser without.

Autumn thinks it can love the world a little longer,
holding out the hope that brilliance in becoming

is no sin, that the colours in the falling leaves
are a form of faith, a means of giving thanks to us

for having each other without fail another year.
It is the hand we feel on the backs of our necks

still partially warm to the touch yet elderly,
a wisdom we sense when the trees stand more upright

as they lose the beauty they spent their lives creating.
Autumn is the grandparent who taught us dignity.

[Love Letter]

The moon came up and I wanted you to see it.
It placed itself in the sky, a face against our window,

reminding me of our baby's head, and smiled at us
when we framed it with love, a small masterpiece.

Bright sky to read by, background of a moment
that in memory is an instant filled with stars

coming to us like the little sounds she made
stirring in her crib, the gentle cry of displeasure

as if a dream foreshadowed her new world
and we soothed her until it was hers again.

And just as a cloud slides past the moon's face
and the rabbit of the skies scampers off to hide,

the light grows older and more distant each day,
until she waves goodbye in the enormous sky.

[Lunar]

In the morning, after the cold and heavy rain,
the park across the street is suddenly stripped

as if the night has eaten its flesh to the bone
and left the penitent shivering to be absolved.

I could forgive the world for what it has done
to another season if only I could not forget

light reflected on your cheeks that shone
with rippled beauty, the softness where I laid

a kiss, your hand wet and cold from testing
the golden glow that resonated from the depths

where minnows swam. I shall go on resisting
change, for life is a sonnet where the truth

is whispered softly, the little sound that pours
into the world like water or love, and always ours.

[After an October Night]

Brown leaves are paper thin beneath our feet.
With every step—listen—you can hear words

gasp because they cannot describe the sky,
the blue as clear as fact that came so honestly

they wound us with their dry semantics.
These are old words. They are written in books

that have yellowed and fallen out of favour,
yesterday's rave reviews, the cocktail parties,

the expectant notices, all crumbling to silence.
They are the praises someone sings before the fall

and each step on brown leaves a small part
of the library of our experience that vanishes

into the open night, wordless, its mouth a maw
waiting to catch its breath, our famous last words.

[Antiquarian Bookshop]

Your hand is cold tonight and the sky
is filled with lost thoughts of a Creator:

streets of cities we dreamed of seeing,
faces of children named but never made,

seem so remote now, wishes unanswered,
possibilities no longer able to hear us calling.

They say prayers rise up on wings and fly
farther than any soul can reach with song.

They say we live in gravity because hope
is lighter than air and outstrips our reach.

Maybe the constellations will reach down
and let us feed them like hungry deer.

Come, hold my hand and let me warm you.
We have fire in our palms to sustain the stars.

[Astronomy]

We are one soul built from a solemn vow,
a tree whose branches reach beyond us,

a place that maps cannot contain, existing
in both shadows and sunlight, the music

of wind that makes our lives speak the love
of life together growing brighter as we grow.

To be one is to offer shade to others on days
when sun bakes the earth and air lingers

waiting for a passing breath to give it voice.
To be one is to fill the air with life magnified

as a beacon standing tall across a harvest field
where the farmer has drawn out the soil's life

so others might be fed; and we shelter love
the way a tree guards a nest until hatchlings fly.

[Tree]

Tourists come from all over the world
to celebrate the vibrant death of nature.

They point their cameras as if to write haiku
and attempt to make beauty a souvenir.

But the colour always dies in its own brilliance.
It is never as real as when it is real, never

as beautiful as when I see you emerging
from a gathering of bright golden birches

with one last flower in your hand that frost
overlooked as it flowed through our sleep.

The cold rock I rest against is foreboding.
It knows its cooled igneous will triumph.

In the meantime, purple aster clings to you,
draws life from you the way a bee drinks nectar.

[The Change]

Leaves that crunch beneath our footsteps
are words that have fallen in the silences

between us. They are brightly coloured,
yellow, red, soft gold, and sunset orange.

They are words that form clever disguises,
covering the place where even shadows fade.

They keep their secrets. They mask our trails.
Listen. The wind is moving through thin arms

that rise and try to touch the sky with need.
They are hands that long for other hands,

fingers curling around the dwindling light.
So many words seem to have died in silence.

So many brightly coloured hopes lie scattered.
Watch where you walk. There is life in them still.

[Words]

The beauty of dictionaries is how they keep
words in order the way a mind or heart

never could. They never stutter, never pause
to consider a better word, or whether what one says

is the right thing to say. A dictionary
has no regrets—one word is neatly placed

with other words of kind until they say
everything that could be said though

it makes no sense except alphabetical sense
and even a staggering statement as that

leaves something to be desired; for what
is desired is the desire that inhabits words

the way pages flutter and reach for air
if left open, their meanings pressed, to fly away.

☛ [Lexicography]

Just as the children removed their masks
so their spirits would not be carried off

and the restless ghosts could be appeased
with sweets we offered to guard our house,

the snow fell. The falling always marks
a threshold. Soon we will be prisoners here.

I felt a small part of my soul fall with one
last leaf from our garden's oak; and if I love

the softness of your skin, the glowing warmth
of your hand in mine, the smile that resists

the chill wind that would make us shelter
or the laughter louder than cold rain falling,

then I would be nothing, helpless, a naked fool.
You clothe me. I go into the night unafraid.

[Ghosts]

Last spring we sat in the darkened church
after the light was passed from hand to hand

and a ticking spoke the world back to life.
Now, this day of saints, this day when darkness

spreads over the fallen world and our cry for life
rises into the snowy night where our words

are beaten back by falling snow, we name them,
speak their prayers into the vast and endless heart

that beats in time to the world, and know
forgiveness is possible; that grace is there for us

if only we have courage to seek it; a journey
undertaken in the dead of winter; a love

felt so deeply in our words and deeds only time
would challenge it. This is the litany of my heart.

[All Saints Day]

With first snow we face the old face of weather.
It haunts us as it did when we were children,

the cold rain of mid-weather and wet snow,
the ground as muddy as late March, the air

heavy with the musk of orange leaves browning
and decaying invisibly before our eyes.

Days fall from heaven and cling to our faces.
They slow us in our travels and remind us

that despite the warmth of summer we are mortal
and the days are cold. You put on the gas fire.

The family room and kitchen become human,
and when I close my eyes I think of sunshine

and imagine it is still there behind the silver,
waiting for you to come home and the door to open.

The night wandered into our lives,
a sad exile in search of the salt bread

of strangers whose winding stairs turn
in the opposite direction of the world.

This night begs to quench its thirst,
touches us with the desire to learn more

than the sound of leaves falling from oaks,
more than the knowledge of touch returned,

the kiss that is a bridge between words,
the sphere where love is a blinding light,

woven in an old blanket to cover us,
as we lie exiled from each other, the warmth

of a hand upon my arm, my hand on your back,
and draw so close there are no more roads.

[The Exile]

Come into this womb of silence—
this puzzle you must solve daily

wherever you rest your tired head.
The journey is continuous, the pathways

endless, and the corridors are infinite.
Here you must stay. Try to be brave.

You have given me a gift to find my way,
a thread from your heart so I can find you.

I know that daylight will unite us,
that courage and our touch in a place

so nameless and remote is what protects us.
We are heroes in a mortal mythology,

and this passage through our winding days
is not merely life but the stuff of legends.

[Hotel II]

Such times as we declare our choices
are seldom moments to consider love,

yet we are the product of a secret ballot,
the vote the heart casts for a future,

a wish for a government of grace.
I campaigned for you, wooed you, courted

your decision until you said yes.
And now, having chosen each other,

having made promises and kept them,
we pass such legislation as to bring

about a world we sorely crave.
Our term, sadly, is but a few years,

and life sits in loyal opposition
as we table amendments to the laws of time.

[The Elect]

The small grey barn owl we discovered
on the branch of our Norwegian pine

studied us but dared not move a feather,
looked deeply into our souls with eyes

that reminded me of two solar eclipses,
the startling realization the light of life

might suddenly disappear from heaven
as if wisdom was as limited as hope.

I have listened long and hard to the silence
that your wise eyes speak when I wake

in the darkness of an autumn night and know
what lies behind them knows me, knows love.

Staring into those eyes is beyond knowing
what it is to be frightened yet not afraid.

[Wisdom]

We enclose the flame by joining hands around the fire.
We enclose the flame to hold the life within us.

We enclose the flame because sparks ascend to stars.
We enclose the flame because the cosmos dwells in us.

We enclose the flame because we want to carry warmth,
and the long winter nights ahead will offer only voices

where our promises rise to fill the sky above us
and we cannot count them for the vastness of love.

We enclose the flame because it holds so many memories,
because the days that encircled each ring in a log

joined hands around the trees that held our hearts,
and time layered itself like fire dwellers joining hands.

And it embraced us like a mother holds her child.
We enclose the flames so our dreams will not escape.

[Keepers of the Flame]

Poets considered time their greatest enemy,
felt the naked entropy of life in their hands

and the rushing decay of beauty like water
flowing through their fingers in frail ink.

But as we live we know the world and time
will go on without us and we feel no animosity

for those things we merely visit with our days.
The enemy is in us, my love, our blind resistance

to love, our sad dedication to daily obligations.
The dust always settles. I wrote these lines in it.

Let us call a truce with ourselves. Let us make
a quiet kingdom where you are my eternal queen

and dwindling daylight gives us time to dream.
That touch of forever is heaven in your kiss.

[Daylight Savings]

There shall be no funerals for life in the record
of our lives as long as I can reach and touch

your hand as we sleep the way fingers of a branch
rise up to touch the moon through clouds.

There shall be feasts we spread before each other,
apples and honey from our best hours shared

the way our hearts evoke the poetry of love in life
and sing quietly to each other in looks and deeds

when the world will not give us time to speak;
we shall have plenty even when our table is bare,

and all may enter in our house to eat their fill.
There shall be desire when the land is lifeless

and hope when nights are lonely as the stars
to be wished on by those who we have touched.

[Touch]

The seasons will go on without us
and other poets will speak of love

with the enormity of the universe
pressed against their ears as seashells

or cocked to windows as snow falls
and silence covers their time with mystery.

We shall be forgotten the way sleep
makes us forget the wonder of living,

yet it will not matter to us then—
these words are echoes repeated to a fade …

for we have had our say, our words,
our time for speaking, our moments of light,

and through it all were true to this ideal:
to be is to live and to live is to love.

[Seasons]

Acknowledgements

I would like to thank Kent Smith for his kindness in letting me use his cottage at Brandy Lake in the summer of 2013 in order to pull this collection of disparate pieces together. The calm, the lake, the blue jays, were very much appreciated. I would also like to thank Earlene Angevine for the use of her elegant and quiet home on Manitoulin Island in the summer of 2013 for the peace and calm to make the necessary editorial changes to the collection. Thank you to Tim and Elke Inkster of the Porcupine's Quill for believing in this book and to Chandra Wohleber for her fine editorial eye. And, a special thank-you to my daughter, Katie, for permitting me to record the moments when they happened. Thank you to Margaret Meyer and Carolyn Meyer also. And to Kerry: these are for you, your green eyes, and your smile.

B.M., September 2013

About the Author

Bruce Meyer is the author of numerous books of poetry, short fiction, non-fiction, pedagogy and literary journalism. His broadcasts on *The Great Books* became the CBC's bestselling spoken-word audio series, and evolved into the national bestseller *The Golden Thread: A Reader's Journey Through the Great Books*. He is professor of English at Georgian College, and teaches for Laurentian University, and Victoria College in the University of Toronto. He is the inaugural Poet Laureate of the City of Barrie, and lives in Barrie, Ontario, with his wife and daughter.

About the Type

In 1926, under the direction of Heinrich Jost, Louis Höll cut the punches for a new version of Bodoni to be offered for sale by the storied Bauer typefoundry of Frankfurt am Main. Bodoni was originally designed by and named after Giambattista Bodoni of Parma, Italy, who designed his famous types at the end of the eighteenth century. Bauer Bodoni is thought to be closest to the original Bodoni both in its proportions and in its characteristic refinement and delicacy. Bodoni is one of the signifiers of the so-called modern style of type design, with its characteristic difference in thick and thin letter strokes, severe vertical stress, and extremely fine, delicate serifs and hairlines.